*The Story of a Special Day*
*Volume 305*

# October
# 31

304th day of the year (305th in leap years). There are
61 days remaining until the end of the year.

by Michael Dobson

Timespinner
Press

This book is also available in e-book form for Kindle, e-pub
devices, and other formats from your favorite online booksellers.

For more information about the series, about us, or about your
special day, please email us at editor@timespinnerpress.com.

Look for other volumes in *The Story of a Special Day,* coming
often. See www.timespinnerpress.com for details and for the most
recent information.

# Table of Contents

**For the definition of "O.S.," "CE," and "BCE" used with some dates , see the section "On Names and Dates."**

**Cover:** A Halloween pumpkin lamp on the cover, by Bojan Cvetanović—the EVENT OF THE DAY.

A
HALLOWE'EN
WISH

ON HALLOWE'EN YOUR SLIGHTEST WISH
IS LIKELY TO COME TRUE,
SO BE CAREFUL, OR THE GOBELINS
WILL SPOIL YOUR WISH FOR YOU.

# HALLOWEEN

EVENT OF THE DAY

October 31 is Halloween, a night of costumes, trick-or-treating, pumpkin carving, and many other activities, beloved by children and adults alike in many countries throughout the world.

**The Origins of Halloween**

Halloween is properly written as Hallowe'en, which is short for Hallowed Evening. In western Christianity, it is the first of three holy days known as "Allhallowtide," or sometimes "Hallowmas."

Some historians believe that the roots of Halloween go back to the Celtic harvest festival of Samhain. As Christianity spread through Europe, many local customs and folk beliefs were integrated into the new religion.

Both the Celts and the newer Christians believed that the end of fall and the beginning of winter was a time when the boundary between this world and the next thinned.

That's why Hallowmas is considered a time to remember the dead. The vigil of Halloween is followed by All Saints' Day, honoring saints and martyrs, and All Souls' Day, remembering the faithful departed, including loved ones.

**From Souling to Trick-or-Treating**

What eventually became trick-or-treating was originally known as *souling*, in which people in disguise would go from house to house, reciting verses or saying prayers for those who gave them money or food. When children became involved, the practice became known as *guising* (disguising). Guising was about treats, but not tricks.

What we know today as trick-or-treating didn't start in the US until the late 1920s and wasn't really popular until after World War II. The "trick" part has always been controversial, even though it's usually not meant seriously; newspapers of the time compared it to extortion.

## Costumes and Jack-o'-Lanterns

Celtics and early Christians believed that on Halloween the souls of the dead returned home for a single night. If you wore a disguise, you could protect yourself from the spirits of the dead, which is where the custom of wearing costumes began.

In some churches, parishioners would dress as saints; elsewhere people dressed as supernatural creatures because of the association with death.

In early America, Anglican colonists in the South and Catholics in Maryland honored All Hallows' Eve, but New England Puritans condemned it. (They also forbade the celebration of Christmas in some areas.)

Certain symbols and traditions of Halloween go far back in time. The Jack-o'-lantern frightened off evil spirit. In Ireland and Scotland, Jack-o'-lanterns were made by carving turnips, but immigrants to North America substituted the native pumpkin.

## Halloween Around the World

In the US, trick-or-treating normally takes place in the evening, but customs vary. In St. Louis, children are asked to perform a joke (the trick) before receiving the candy (treat). In parts of Canada, people say "Halloween apples" instead of "Trick-or-treat." In French-speaking neighborhoods of Quebec, children used to say, "La charité s'il-vous-plaît," or "Charity, please."

In Portugal, children go out in the daytime on either All Saints' Day or All Souls' Day. In Sweden, the day for trick-or-treating is Maundy Thursday, the Thursday before Easter; the Danes go out on Shrove Monday, the Monday before Ash Wednesday; and in Finland it's Palm Sunday.

In parts of the Netherlands, Germany, Switzerland, and Austria, children go door to door on St. Martin's Day, November 11; in northern Germany and southern Denmark, it's celebrated as *Rummelpott* on New Year's Eve.

Parties and games are also common on Halloween, with such traditional activities as dunking for apples, telling ghost stories, and creating haunted houses, corn mazes, and hayrides.

Some Jewish, Muslim, and Protestant denominations forbid the celebration of Halloween.

Although Halloween is primarily European in origin, the custom of dressing in costumes and going trick-or-treating has spread throughout the world.

# MORE 10/31 HOLIDAYS

### Eve of Winter Celebrations

A number of other celebrations take place on Halloween, which in many Northern Hemisphere cultures is considered the eve of the first day of winter.

- Allantide (Cornwall, England)
- Hop-tu-Naa (Isle of Man)
- Samhain (Celtic cultures and Neopagans)
- Beltane (in the Southern Hemisphere)
- Day of the Dead (first day, Mexico)

### Día de la Canción Criolla (Peru)

Celebrating the *criolla* culture of Peru.

### Rashtriya Ekta Diwas (National Unity Day) (India)

Celebrates the integration of over 550 independent princely states into the nation of India.

### World Savings Day

Promotes the saving of money, especially in developing countries.

Day of the Dead Musicians (Musical Instrument Museum, Phoenix)

## National Caramel Apple Day (United States)

In the United States, almost every day of the year is dedicated to a particular food. Sponsored by manufacturers, retailers, farmers, or simply fans, these days are often proclaimed by the President, Congress, state governors, or mayors. Given that there are more different foods than days of the year, some days honor more than one kind of food!

October 31 is National Caramel Apple Day, in honor of the traditional Halloween treat—though they're tasty every day of the year.

## October Food Holidays

The entire month of October is used to celebrate numerous foods. Here's a list of what to eat in the month of October!

- National Apple Month
- National Applejack Month
- National Caramel Month
- National Cookbook Month
- National Cookie Month
- National Dessert Month
- National Pasta Month
- National Pickled Peppers Month
- National Pizza Month
- National Popcorn Poppin' Month
- National Pork Month
- National Pretzel Month
- National Seafood Month

## Christian Feast Days

Each day in the year is considered a feast day for one or more saints. They are somewhat different in western Christianity (Catholicism and many forms of Protestantism) and in eastern (Orthodox) Christianity.

Martin Luther, by Lucas Cranach the Elder

In *Western Christianity*, Alphonsus Rodriguez, Blessed Theodore Romzha (Ruthenian Catholic Church), *Martin Luther* (Anglican Communion), Paul Shinji Sasaki and Philip Lindel Tsen (Episcopal Church), Quentin, and Wolfgang of Regensburg are commemorated on October 31.

In *Eastern Orthodox Christianity*, it is the commemoration of the Apostles of the Seventy, Saint Maura of Constantinople, Saint Jacob of Nisibis, the Holy Twelve Daughters, the Holy Three Martyrs of Melitene, and the Holy Child Martyr. (These are observed on October 18 by "Old Calendarists;" fixed commemorations are observed on November 13.)

## Other Holidays

Some holidays are simply made up by individuals, companies, or other organizations, and whether they become widely adopted depends on whether people choose to celebrate them. Here are some opportunities to celebrate on October 31.

October 31 is:
- Beggars' Night,
- Books for Treats Day
- Day of the Seven Billion
- Girl Scout Founder's Day
- National Knock-Knock Jokes Day
- *National Magic Day*
- World Cities Day

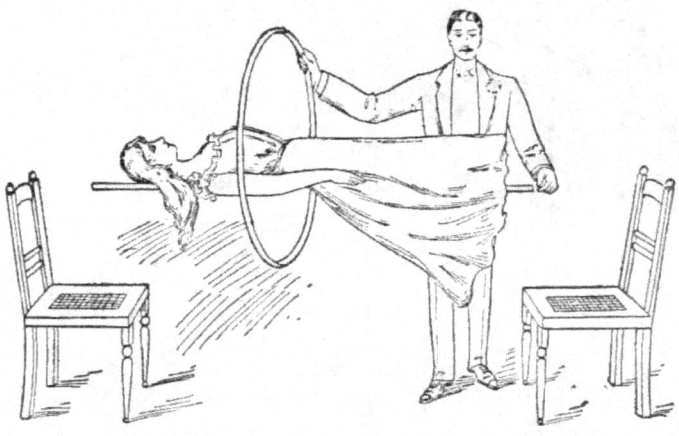

Illustration from *Magic*, by Ellis Stanyon (1910)

# TODAY IN HISTORY
# OCTOBER 31

Detail from a painting of Martin Luther
nailing his 95 theses to the church door, by Julius Hübner (1878)

9

## 1517 – Martin Luther Releases the 95 Theses/The Protestant Reformation Begins

On October 31, 1517, German priest Martin Luther sent 95 *theses*, or arguments, to the Archbishop of Mainz, criticizing the practice by priests of selling certificates that would reduce the punishment for sins, known as *indulgences*. This triggered a major controversy in the Catholic Church that began the Protestant Reformation in Europe. This date is often cited as the official beginning of the Reformation. It's often stated that Luther nailed the 95 theses to the door of his church, but this is uncertain — and if he did, it was likely in mid-November, not October 31.

## 1922 – Mussolini Takes Power

On October 31, 1922, Italian fascist leader Benito Mussolini became Prime Minister of Italy. Three years after becoming Prime Minister, he established a legal dictatorship, taking on the new role of *Il Duce* (The Leader), and ruled the country until he was deposed in 1943.

Benito Mussolini

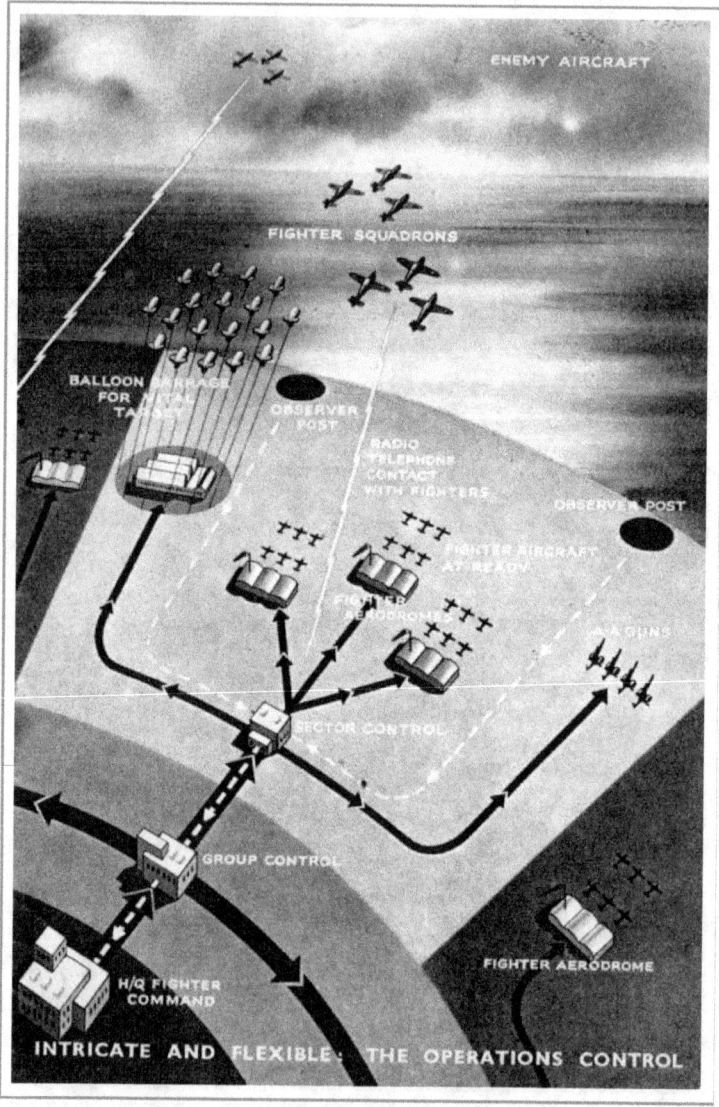

From a 1941 pamphlet published by the UK Air Minstry, describing operations control during the Battle of Britain

## 1940 – The Battle of Britain Ends

The Battle of Britain, the first major campaign in world history to be fought entirely by air forces, took place from July 10 to October 31, 1940, according to most British historians. (German historians generally regard the campaign as lasting until June 1941.) Pitting the Royal Air Force against the Luftwaffe, the British lost over 1,600 aircraft of a total force of just under 2,000, while the Germans lost nearly 2,000 aircraft out of some 2,500 total planes. In addition to 1,500 British and 2,600 German aviators losing their lives, there were over 40,000 civilian deaths, mostly from bombing.

Prime Minister Winston Churchill praised the pilots and crew, saying, "if the British Empire and its Commonwealth lasts for a thousand years, men will still say, 'This was their finest hour.'"

## 1941 – Mt. Rushmore Completed

The famous Mount Rushmore National Memorial, a giant sculpture of four US presidents carved into the face of Mount Rushmore, located in Keystone, South Dakota. The heads of George Washington, Thomas Jefferson, Theodore Roosevelt, and Abraham Lincoln are each 60 feet in eight, with the entire memorial covering nearly two square miles.

The idea of creating giant sculptures in the Black Hills region is credited to historian Doane Robinson, who originally intended the sculpture to feature Western heroes. Sculptor Gutzon Borglum, hired to do the project, argued it should have a more national focus, and chose the four presidents portrayed. Construction began in 1927, and was completed on October 31, 1941, seven months after Gutzon Borglum's death.

An iconic symbol of the United States, Mount Rushmore attracts over 2 million visitors each year.

Workers doing seasonal maintenance
on Mt. Rushmore (Photo: Jeff Waddell)

# OTHER OCTOBER 31 EVENTS

*1864* — Nevada becomes the 36th US state.

*1876* — A monster cyclone kills over 200,000 people in India..

*1903* — The "Purdue Wreck," a train collision in Indianapolis, kills 17, including 14 members of the Purdue football team.

*1913* — The Lincoln Highway, the first automobile highway across the United States, is dedicated.

*1917*— World War I's **Battle of Beersheba**, sometimes called "the last successful cavalry charge in history," takes place.

*1918* — The Austro-Hungarian Empire is dissolved.

*1961* — Joseph Stalin's body is removed from Vladimir Lenin's tomb in Moscow.

*2000* — Soyuz TM-31, carrying the first resident crew of the International Space Station, is launched.

*2014* — Virgin Galactic's SpaceShipTwo crashes in the Mojave Desert.

Turkish lancers west of Beersheba in Ottoman Palestine (1917)

Original manuscript of "On Looking Into
Chapman's Homer" by John Keats

# OCTOBER 31
# BIRTHDAYS

Portrait of John Keats, by William Hilton the Younger
John Keats was born October 31, 1795

### John Candy (October 31, 1950 — March 4, 1994)

Canadian comedian and actor John Candy began his career with the Second City comedy troupe in Toronto, and gained fame as a cast member of the television show SCTV. He appeared in over 40 films including *Stripes*, *Spaceballs*, and *Planes, Trains and Automobiles*. He died at the age of 43 of a heart attack.

### Jane Pauley (October 31, 1950 — )

Television journalist Jane Pauley was co-host of NBC's *The Today Show* for 13 years, and subsequently co-host of *Dateline NBC* for 12 years, for which she won numerous awards. She married *Doonesbury* cartoonist Garry Trudeau in 1980.

### Brian Piccolo (October 31, 1943 — June 16, 1970)

Chicago Bears running back Brian Piccolo died at the age of 26 from an aggressive form of cancer. He was the subject of the 1971 film *Brian's Song*, remade in 2001.

Brian Piccolo

Michael Landon

## Michael Landon (October 31, 1936 — July 1, 1991)

Actor, writer, director, and producer Michael Landon (Eugene Maurice Orowitz) gained fame for his role as Little Joe on the long-running Western show *Bonanza* from 1959 to 1973. He then played Charles Ingalls in *Little House on the Prairie*, also serving as executive producer, writer, and director, from 1974 to 1983, and as probationary angel Jonathan Smith in *Highway to Heaven* until his death from cancer at the age of 54.

## Dan Rather (October 31, 1931 — )

Television journalist Dan Rather was managing editor and anchor of *CBS Evening News* for 24 years, and regularly contributed to the news magazine *60 Minutes*. A member of the Television Hall of Fame, Rather won seven Peabody Awards and numerous Emmys during his long career.

## Michael Collins (October 31, 1930 — )

Astronaut Michael Collins was command module pilot of Apollo 11, the first spacecraft to reach the Moon, remaining in orbit while crewmates Neil Armstrong and Buzz Aldrin made the first manned landing on the Moon's surface. He was previously pilot of the Gemini 10 mission, where he became the first person to perform two extravehicular activities (EVAs). Following his years with NASA, he became director of the Smithsonian Institution's National Air and Space Museum.

Astronaut Mike Collins suits up for the Apollo 11 mission

## Dale Evans (October 31, 1912 — February 7, 2001)

Dale Evans was the wife of Western film legend Roy Rogers, and co-starred in more than 30 films and in the hit TV series The Roy Rogers Show. She wrote Roy Rogers' theme song, "Happy Trails."

## Chiang Kai-shek (October 31, 1887 — April 5, 1975)

Chinese political and military leader Chiang Kai-shek (蔣中正) was integral in the formation of the Republic of China, which ruled from 1928 to 1948, when the Communist People's Republic of China took power on the mainland. The Republic of China's government and military retreated to Taiwan, where Chiang Kai-shek ruled until his death in 1975.

Dale Evans (right) with Roy Rogers

## Juliette Gordon Low (October 31, 1860 — January 17, 1927)

Juliette Gordon Low founded what became the Girl Scouts of the United States of America. Working with the founder of Scouting, British general Robert Baden-Powell, she organized the original troop of Girl Guides of America in Savannah, Georgia, on March 12, 1912. (The name changed to Girl Scouts the following year.) Through her tireless efforts, Girl Scouting expanded in the United States, and now has more than 2.3 million members.

## John Keats (October 31, 1795 — February 23, 1821)

One of the most beloved figures in Romantic poetry, John Keats wrote poetry seriously for only six years before his early death from tuberculosis at the age of 25. His most famous works include "Ode on a Grecian Urn," "On First Looking Into Chapman's Homer," and "La Belle Dame sans Merci."

Juliette Gordon Low

Singer Ethel Waters, born October 31, 1896
(Photo: William P. Gottlieb)

# MORE OCTOBER 31
# BIRTHDAYS

### Business

**Eugene Meyer**, publisher of the Washington Post, Chairman of the Federal Reserve, first President of the World Bank (1875)

### Chess

**Alexander Alekhine**, world chess champion, considered one of the greatest chess players of all time (1892)

### Government

**Reza Pahlavi**, crown prince of Iran (1960)

**Vallabhbhai Patel**, a founding father of the Republic of India, often called *Sardar,* or Chief. (1875)

### Letters

**Neil Stephenson,** science fiction writer (1959)

**Katherine Paterson**, children's novelist, wrote *Bridge to Terabithia* (1932)

**Andrew Sarris,** film critic (1928)

**Dick Francis,** steeplechase jockey and mystery writer (1920)

**B. H. Liddell Hart**, military historian and theorist (1895)

## Military

**Boston Custer,** youngest brother of George Armstrong Custer; died at Little Big Horn (1848)

## Music

**Willow Smith**, singer and actress, known for "Whip My Hair," daughter of actors Will Smith and Jada Pinkett Smith (2000)

**Linn Berggren**, singer for Ace of Base (1970)

**Adam Schlesinger,** known for Fountains of Wayne and other acts (1967)

**Vanilla Ice** (Robert Van Winkle), rapper and actor (1967)

**Annabella Lwin**, lead singer of Bow Wow Wow (1966)

**Ad-Rock** (Adam Horovitz), rapper known for Beastie Boys (1966)

**Darryl Worley**, country music artist (1964)

**Johnny Marr**, guitarist and co-songwriter for The Smiths (1963)

**Mikkey Dee,** drummer for Motörhead (1963)

**Raphael Rabello,** Brazilian guitarist (1962)

**Larry Mullen Jr.,** drummer for U2 (1961)

**Brian Stokes Mitchell**, singer and actor, won a Tony in 2000 for *Kiss Me, Kate* (1957)

**Tom Paxton**, folk singer-songwriter, winner of a Grammy Lifetime Achievement Award (1937)

**Illinois Jacquet**, tenor sax player known for his solo on "Flying Home" (1922)

**Ethel Waters**, jazz and gospel singer known for "Stormy Weather" and "Cabin in the Sky" (1896)

## Performing Arts

**Scott Clifton,** actor known for *General Hospital, One Life to Live,* and *The Bold and the Beautiful* (1984)

**Eddie Kaye Thomas,** actor known for the *American Pie* films and the *Harold & Kumar* series (1980)

**Piper Perabo**, actress known for *Coyote Ugly* and *Covert Affairs* (1976)

**Rob Schneider**, actor and comedian, known for *Saturday Night Live* and for such films as *Deuce Bigalow: Male Gigolo* (1963)

**Dermot Mulroney,** actor known for *Young Guns* and *My Best Friend's Wedding* (1963)

**Peter Jackson**, New Zealand filmmaker, director and producer of *The Lord of the Rings* film trilogy (1961)

**Ken Wahl**, actor known for *Wiseguy* (1954 or 1957)

**Michael J. Anderson**, actor known for *Twin Peaks* (1953)

**Michael Kitchen**, actor, known for roles in the TV series *Foyle's War* and two James Bond films (1948)

**Deirdre Hall**, actress known for *Days of Our Lives* (1947)

**Stephen Rea**, Irish film actor, nominated for an Academy Award for *The Crying Game* (1946)

**Norman Lovett**, actor and comedian, known for *Red Dwarf* (1946)

**Brian Doyle-Murray**, actor and comedian, brother of Bill Murray (1945)

**Sally Kirkland**, actress, nominated for an Academy Award for *Anna* (1941)

**David Ogden Stiers**, played Major Winchester on *M\*A\*S\*H* (1942)

**Ron Rifkin**, actor known for *Alias* and *Brothers & Sisters* (1939)

**Tom O'Connor,** game show host (1939)

**Bud Spencer** (Carlo Pedersoli), Italian actor, filmmaker, and professional swimmer (1929)

**Jimmy Savile**, English DJ and television personality, host of the BBC show *Top of the Pops* (1926)

**Cleo Moore**, actress and pin-up girl (1924)

**Barbara Bel Geddes,** actress known for roles in the TV series *Dallas* and the Hitchcock film *Vertigo* (1922)

**John Sylvester-White,** actor, known for *Search for Tomorrow* and *Welcome Back, Kotter* (1919)

**Ollie Johnson,** animator, one of Disney's Nine Old Men, winner of the National Medal of Arts (1912)

## Politics and Government

**Norodom Sihanouk**, King of Cambodia, later Prime Minister following his abdication (1922)

## Science

**Sir John Pople**, Nobel Prize winner in Chemistry (1925)

**Adolf von Baeyer,** Nobel Prize winner in Chemistry (1835)

## Sports

**Alphonso Ford**, basketball player known as one of the greatest scorers in college basketball history (1971)

**Steve Trachsel,** baseball pitcher known as "The Human Rain Delay" (1970)

**Buddy Lazier,** racing driver, winner of the 1996 Indianapolis 500 (1967)

**Alonzo Babers**, Olympic gold medalist in relay (1961)

**Jeannie Longo**, French racing cyclist, 13-time World Champion (1958)

**Nick Saban**, football coach, named "The Most Powerful Coach in Sports" by *Forbes* in 2008 (1951)

**Frank Shorter,** long-distance runner, Olympic gold medalist (1947)

**Derek Bell**, British Formula One race car driver (1941)

**Dale Brown**, basketball coach for the LSU Tigers (1935)

**Newsy Lalonde**, hockey and lacrosse player, member of the Hockey Hall of Fame (1887)

## Visual Arts

**Helmut Newton**, photographer (1920)

# CHALLENGE
## TO
# HOUDINI

## REGENT THEATRE, SALFORD.

Dear Sir,

We, the undersigned Committee, as the result of a controversy, have purchased from the **Henshaw Blind Asylum,** Stretford Road, one of their Extra Strong and Large Travelling Baskets, and Challenge you to allow us to Lock, Chain, and Rope you in the Basket, and defy you to make your Escape. Test to be made at the Residence of any one of the Committee you may select.

Awaiting your reply, yours truly,

HENRY HAVLIN, 255 Eccles New Road, Salford.
J. N. F. CARSIDE, 25 Eccles New Road, Salford.
J. CROOK & SONS, Regent Road, Salford.
IRWIN BROOK, 35 Trafford Road, Salford.
C. W. KIRKBRIDE, 160 Regent Road, Salford.

**HOUDINI** accepts no test to take place privately, and requests the Gentlemen to bring the Hamper to

# REGENT THEATRE
### SALFORD,
## SECOND HOUSE,
# FRIDAY, JAN. 22ND.

**HOUDINI** will forfeit **£50** to anyone who can find any False Means or Exits, or Traps in the Basket.

JOHN HEYWOOD, Ltd., Printers, Manchester.

Harry Houdini, died October 31, 1926

### Federico Fellini (January 20, 1920 — October 31, 1993)

Known as one of the most influential filmmakers of all time, Italian director Federico Fellini's best known films include *La Dolce Vita, 8-1/2, La Strada,* and *Juliet of the Spirits.* His films won four Academy Awards and he was awarded an honorary Oscar for Lifetime Achievement.

### Indira Gandhi (November 19, 1917 — October 31, 1984)

Indira Gandhi was the first (and so far only) woman to be Prime Minister of India. She served in that office for fifteen years until her assassination in 1984. The daughter of Indian independence figure and first prime minister Jawaharlal Nehru, Indira's time in office is second only to her father. She was succeeded as prime minister by her son, Rajiv Gandhi.

Indira Gandhi

## Harry Houdini (March 24, 1874 — October 31, 1926)

Perhaps the best known illusionist and escape artist ever, Harry Houdini (born Erik Weisz) was known for his sensational escape acts. In addition, he was president of the Society of American Magicians and an active debunker of spiritualists. He appeared un several films. He was also an aviation pioneer, and is often (incorrectly) credited as being the first person to fly in Australia. He died of peritonitis, possibly after being repeatedly punched in the stomach. His brother, Thomas Hardeen, inherited his props and continued the act.

Harry Houdini, circa 1898

## Business

**Egon Schiele**, major figurative painter of the early 20th century (1875)

## Letters

**Studs Terkel**, historian and broadcaster; won the Pulitzer Prize in 1985 for *The Good War* (2008)

**Ring Lardner, Jr.**, journalist and screenwriter blacklisted during the post-World War II Red Scare period (1986)

## Military and Government

**Ted Sorensen**, advisor and speechwriter to President John F. Kennedy (2010)

**P. W. Botha**, prime minister and State President of South Africa prior to the end of apartheid; known as *Die Groot Krokodil*, or "The Big Crocodile" (2006)

**Joseph Hooker**, Union general during the American Civil War (1879)

## Performing Arts

**Rosalind Cash**, played Mary Mae Ward on *General Hospital* and Charlton Heston's love interest in 1971's *The Omega Man* (1983)

**River Phoenix**, actor known for such films as Stand By Me, Running on Empty, and My Own Private Idaho; died of drug-related heart failure (1993)

**Joseph Papp**, theatrical producer and director known for the formation of New York's The Public Theater and for his Shakespeare in the Park outdoor festival (1991)

**John Houseman**, actor best remembered for his role in the film and TV series *The Paper Chase*, also known for his long collaboration with Orson Welles (1988)

---

**Max Linder**, French actor, director, and producer during the silent film era, known as "the first international movie star" (1925)

---

## Science

**Robert S. Mulliken**, won the Nobel Prize for Chemistry for his work in molecular orbital theory (1986)

## Sports

**George Halas**, known as "Papa Bear" and "Mr. Everything," was a co-founder of the NFL and founder and owner of the Chicago Bears (1983)

**Bill Durnan**, hockey player, two-time Stanley Cup winner and member of the Hockey Hall of Fame (1972)

## Religion

**Charles Taze Russell**, founded *The Watch Tower*, which led to the development of Jehovah's Witnesses and other groups affiliated with the Bible Student movement (1916)

Poster for tm *Seven Years Bad Luck* (1921)
starring Max Linder, who died October 31, 1925

*October*, by Hans Thoma

# THE TENTH MONTH
# OCTOBER

*October*, by Eugène Grasset

*October*, by Joachim von Sandrart

# ABOUT THE MONTH OF
# O C T O B E R

*"I'm so glad I live in a world where there are Octobers."*
— Lucy Maud Montgomery, *Anne of Green Gables*

In Latin, *octo* means eight, so why is October the tenth month? Originally, it was, because the early Roman calendar began the new year in March. What about January and February? They didn't exist, because winter was considered a "monthless" period. It wasn't until 713 BCE that those first two months got added, and October got pushed from $8^{th}$ place to $10^{th}$ in the calendar year.

Whether it's the eighth month or the tenth, October has always had 31 days. The last day of October and the last day of February end on the same day of the week in both regular and leap years.

From a seasonal point of view, October is the second month of autumn in the Northern Hemisphere and the second month of spring in the Southern Hemisphere. It corresponds to April in the other hemisphere.

As an odd bit of trivia, more US presidents have been born in October than in any other month. There are six: John Adams, Rutherford B. Hayes, Chester A. Arthur, Theodore Roosevelt, and Jimmy Carter.

Detail from *October*, from *Très Riches Heures du Duc de Berry* by the Limbourg brothers and Barthélemy d'Eyck.

# OCTOBER IN OTHER
# LANGUAGES

The month of October has different names in different languages. Some are very similar to English (octobre, oktober, etc.), while some are quite different. Some nations use calendars other than the Gregorian, and their months may overlap with October. In lunar-based calendars, such as the Islamic calendar, months move through the seasons, but many of these languages have a word for October.

**Albanian:** Tetor

**Anglo-Saxon:** Wyn-monath (wine month)

**Arabic (Egypt, Sudan, Yemen):** يوناأغينافبرايتشرين (uktūbar) الأأكتوبر

**Arabic (Levant):** حزيركانوشباتشرين الأول (tishrīn al-awwal)

**Arabic (Libya):** الصهناالنالتمور، الثمور (at-tumūr; al-tumūr)

**Arabic (Morocco, Algeria, and Tunisia):** جأيفيفرأكتوبر، أوكتوبر (uktūbər; ūktūbər)

**Azerbaijani:** Oktyabrl

**Basque:** Urri

**Chinese:** 十月 (Cantonese: sahpyuht; Mandarin: shíyuè; Taiwanese: chap-goeh)

**Croatian:** Listopad

**Czech:** říjen

**Finnish:** Lokakuu

**Greek:** Οκτώβριος (Októbrios)

**Haitian Creole:** Oktòb

**Hebrew:** ינפבברואוקטובר (ôqtôber)

**Hind**i: अक्टूबर (aktūbar)

**Irish (Gaelic):** Deireadh Fómhair mí Dheireadh Fómhair

**Italian:** Ottobre

**Japanese (traditional calendar):** 十月 (jūgatsu); 神無月 (kaminaduki)

**Khoekhoe (Nama):** ǂnû ǁǁnâiseb

**Korean**: 시월 (siweol)

**Lithuanian:** Spalis

**Manx:** Jerrey-fouyir

**Maori:** Whiringa ā nuku

**Old English**: Winterfylleþ

**Polish:** Październik

**Quechua:** Kantarayki

**Russian:** октябрь (oktjabr')

**Sardinian:** Ladàmini

**Scottish Gaelic:** an t-Sultain

**Sesotho:** Mphalane

**Spanish**: Febrero

**Swahili:** Oktoba

**Swazi:** iMphala

**Thai:** Tulakhom

**Turkish:** Ekim

**Ukrainian:** жовтень (zhovten)

**Vietnamese:** 腩进 (tháng mười)

**Welsh:** Hydref

**Yiddish:** פֿעברואַאָקטאָבער (oktober)

**Zulu:** uOkthoba

Mengapa?    Zašto?
为什么呢？
Por quê? Чаму?
Чому?
Poukisa? كيون؟    Per què?
Tại sao?  Miks?
Bakit? Kial? למה?
Waarom?    Hvers vegna?
どうして？  פארוואס?    Niyə?
Warum? Dlaczego? Pourquoi?
Ինչու?  Зашто? چرا؟  Quid?
Cén fáth?    Pam?
Zergatik? რატომ?  Miért?
Kwa nini? Proč?
Hoekom?    क्यों?
De ce?    Kodėl?
เพราะเหตุใด  Защо? Why?
Perché?  Miksi?
لماذا؟  Prečo?  Varför?
Γιατί;
Għaliex?  ¿Por qué? Pse?
왜? Почему?  Зошто?
Kāpēc?  Neden?
Hvorfor?  為什麼呢？

# OCTOBER SAYINGS AND
# SUPERSTITIONS

Here are some sayings and superstitions associated with the month of October.

### October Weather Superstitions

Rain in October means wind in December.

When birds and badgers are fat in October, expect a cold winter.

When berries are many in October, beware a hard winter.

If ducks do slide at Hallowtide, at Christmas they will swim; if ducks do swim at Hallowtide, at Christmas they will slide.

There will always be 29 fine days in October.

If the October moon comes without frost, expect no frost till the moon of November.

### October Wedding Superstitions

If in October you do marry, love will come but riches tarry.

The three luckiest months for a wedding are June, October, and December.

An October bride will be pretty, coquettish, loving, but jealous.

Married when leaves in October thin, toil and hardships for you begin.

## Halloween Superstitions

If you see bats flying around your house on Halloween, ghosts and spirits are nearby.

If you go to a crossroads at Halloween and listen to the wind, you will learn all the most important things that will befall you during the next twelve months.

Children born on Halloween are said to have the gift of second sight, and can ward off evil spirits.

If you see a spider on Halloween night, it means the spirit of a departed loved one is watching over you.

If you ring bells on Halloween, you will chase away evil spirits.

And if you want to meet a witch, put your clothes on inside out and walk backwards on Halloween night!

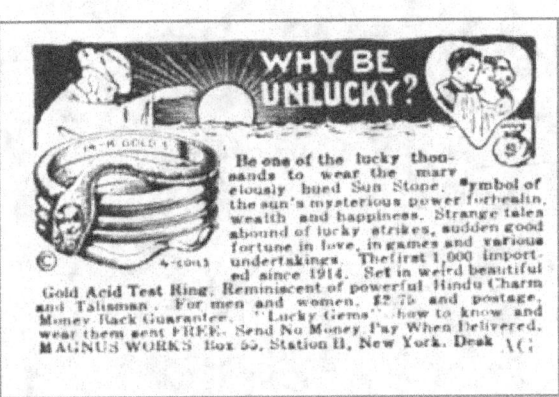

1926 advertisement for lucky jewelry

*Marigolds*, by Dante Gabriel Rossetti

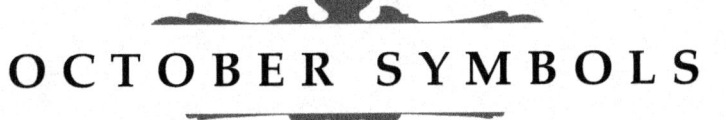

# OCTOBER SYMBOLS

**Birthstones by Culture:** Although a variety of birthstones have been associated with each month, the National Association of Jewelers adopted an official list of stones for each birth month. For October, the stones are *opal* and *tourmaline*.

Other stones associated with October include *aquamarine* and *coral*. There are also birthstones associated with the signs of the zodiac. For October, Libra (9/23-10/23) is associated with *chrysolite*, and Scorpio (10/24-11/21) with *beryl*.

**Birth Flowers**: *Calendula*, also known as *Marigold*, or Cosmos. It is associated with warmth, elegance, and devotion, as well as comfort and healing.

**Birth Tree:** The ancient Druids associated trees with different months of the year. For people born between September 30 and October 27, the birth tree is *ivy*. From October 28 through November 24, it is the *reed*.

# EVENTS IN OCTOBER

## Honorary Months

Presidents, Congresses, and nations around the world issue proclamations recognizing particular months to honor certain causes. These events generally fall in October, though honorary months do come and go. Holidays established by states and nonprofit organizations are listed if verified. If not otherwise specified, all months are US. There is some variation from year to year; some celebratory months get added and others get dropped. Two places to get up to date information are the current edition of *Chase's Calendar of Events* or the website www.brownielocks.com/October.html.

## Culture

- Black History Month (UK)
- Filipino American History Month
- German American Heritage Month (September 15-October 15 in the US)
- Hispanic Heritage Month (September 15-October 15 in the US)
- Italian American Heritage Month
- LGBT History Month
- Polish American Heritage Month

# Food

- American Cheese Month
- Apple Month
- National Pizza Month
- National Popcorn Poppin' Month
- National Pork Month
- National Sausage Month

# Health

- American Pharmacists Month
- Antidepressant Death Awareness Month
- Brain Tumor Awareness Month (Canada)
- Breast Cancer Awareness Month
- Celiac Sprue Awareness Month
- Dental Hygiene Month
- Down Syndrome Awareness Month
- Dwarfism/Little People Awareness Month
- Dyslexia Awareness Month
- Eczema Awareness Month
- Health Literacy Month
- Healthy Lung Month
- Infertility Awareness Month
- Liver Awareness Month
- Lupus Erythematosus Month
- Medical Ultrasound Awareness Month
- Physical Therapy Month
- Rett Syndrome Awareness Month
- Spina Bifida Awareness Month

- Sudden Infant Death Syndrome (SIDS) Awareness Month
- World Blindness Awareness Month

# Other

- Bat Appreciation Month
- Black Speculative Fiction Month
- Caffeine Addiction Recovery Month
- Church Library Month
- Class Reunion Month
- Domestic Violence Awareness Month
- Fair Trade Month
- Feral Hog Month
- Financial Planning Month
- International Walk to School Month
- Month of the Holy Rosary (Catholicism)
- National Adopt a Shelter Dog Month
- National Arts and Humanities Month

# Moveable and Multi-Day Events

Some events take place over a specific week or time period. Start and finish dates may vary from year to year. Some events occur on different days each year (such as "fourth Saturday of a month"). These events sometimes take place on this day.

**Last Friday (10/25-31)**
- Nevada Day (Nevada)
- Teacher's Day (Australia)

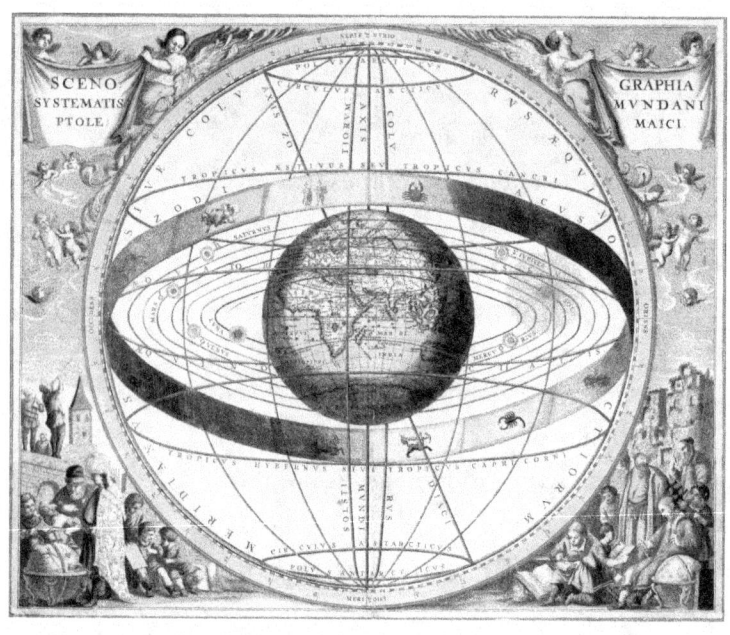

*Scenography of the Ptolemaic Cosmography,* by Johannes van Loon, based on Andreas Cellarius's *Harmonia Macrocosmica,* 1660

# ZODIAC SIGNS
# OCTOBER

From the perspective of someone on Earth, the Sun appears to move through the sky throughout the year, along a path astronomers call the *ecliptic plane*. The ecliptic plane is divided into twelve constellations, known as the zodiac, based on traditionally observed patterns of stars. On your birthday, you can't see your constellation, because it's in the daytime sky.

The zodiac was first developed by Babylonian astronomers about 2,500 years ago. Because they were unaware that the Earth wobbles like a spinning top (known as *precession*), they didn't make allowance for the fact that the Sun's path through the zodiac changes over time.

That means there are now two sets of dates for your birth sign. The *tropical dates* are the original Babylonian dates; the *sidereal dates* tell you where the Sun actually appears as it moves along its annual path.

For October 31, the tropical zodiac sign is **Scorpio** (10/23-11/21), and the sidereal sign is **Libra** (10/16-11/15).

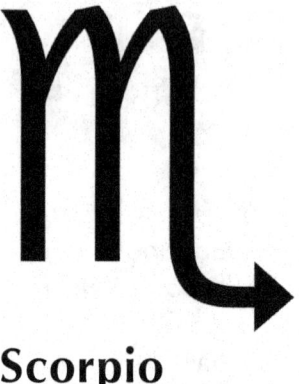

# Scorpio

**Tropical** October 23 to November 21

**Sidereal** November 16 to December 15

Scorpio, the Scorpion, appears in the Greek myth of the hunter Orion. Because Orion had touched the robes of the goddess Artemis, in revenge, the goddess had the scorpion kill Orion. As a reward, she placed the scorpion in the sky, where it chases Orion through the eternal night.

Scorpio is a fire sign, and people born under this sign are supposed to be determined, reserved, loyal, and secretive. Scorpios are supposed to be compatible with the water signs of Pisces and Capricorn.

# Libra

**Tropical** September 23 to October 23

**Sidereal** October 16 to November 15

The Babylonians considered Libra, the Scales, to be sacred to the sun god Shamash, patron of truth and justice. The Romans reassigned the scales to Astraea, the celestial virgin, better known as Virgo.

Libra is an air sign, and people born under this sign are supposed to be extroverts, socially graceful, and just. Librans are supposed to be compatible with the other air signs of Gemini and Aquarius.

Illustration by Edward Penfield

# WHAT DAY OF THE WEEK IS OCTOBER 31?

On what day of the week does October 31 fall?

Surprisingly, this isn't an easy question. Because the calendar year is 365 days long (366 in leap years), it doesn't divide evenly by the seven days of the week.

Also, the Earth goes around the Sun in about 365-1/4 days, so a calendar tends to drift over time. That's why the same date falls on different weekdays in different years.

This is made even more complicated by a change in calendars that took place in 1582. Our modern calendar has its roots in ancient Rome, in a calendar reform conducted by Julius Caesar. Caesar commissioned mathematicians to attack the problem, and they came up with the idea of leap years, and thus standardized the calendar for centuries to come. This was called the Julian calendar.

Over time, however, the small errors in Caesar's calculation compounded. That's why Pope Gregory XIII commissioned the Gregorian calendar, used in most of the world today. Some countries converted in 1582, when the calendar was first developed; some converted later; other still haven't changed.

Gregorian and Julian aren't the only types of calendars. The Hebrew year, the Islamic year, and many other calendars are used in different parts of the world and among different people.

You can convert Gregorian dates to other calendars, including the Hebrew calendar, the Islamic calendar, and even the Mayan calendar by visiting the Fourmilab Calendar Converter at http://www.fourmilab.ch/documents/calendar/.

Chinese calendar systems are quite complex and have changed several times; a full discussion is far beyond the scope of this book. If you're interested, you can find information here: http://www.hermetic.ch/cal_stud/chinese_cal.htm.

# On Names and Dates

Historians use "CE" (Common Era) and "BCE" (Before the Common Era) instead of the more common "AD" (Anno Domini, or Year of Our Lord) and "BC" (Before Christ), reflecting the fact that the year-numbering system established by the Gregorian calendar is used throughout the world in many countries not culturally Christian.

The CE/BCE designation dates back to at least 1708, and has been adopted as a standard by the United Nations and the Universal Postal Union. Because this series of books covers events and people of all nations and cultures, we use the CE/BCE style.

The abbreviation "O.S." ("Old Style") on some dates refers to the fact that not all nations switched from the Julian to the Gregorian calendar at the same time. (The first nations switched in 1582, the Russian

Empire did not do so until 1918.) Therefore some figures and events have two dates, with the Julian date given the "O.S." designation.

Also, in the Julian calendar in England in the 16th century, the year began on March 25 rather than January 1. To avoid confusion with Gregorian dates, dates between January and March were often (but not always) written using both years.

People and events whose original names are not in the Western alphabet have their native names (where possible) in the appropriate script shown in parenthesis. If you are using an e-reader to access an electronic version of this book, all characters don't always display on all devices.

A 50-year brass perpetual calendar.

Cartoon by John T. McCutcheon

# COPYRIGHT, CREDIT, AND CONTACT US

## Follow Us

Our blog "This Day in History" (http://timespinnerpress.com/this-day-in-history/) features short articles on events and people associated with each day, and updates several times each week. Also subscribe to the "Quote of the Day" at http://timespinnerpress.com/quote-of-the-day/. You can get daily links by following us on Facebook at TimespinnerPress, or on Twitter as @sidewisethinker.

## Contact Us

Find an error or a format problem? Want information about the series, about us, or about when the volume for your special day might be available? Please email us at editor@timespinnerpress.com. (We also take requests if your special day isn't yet complete. Please give us at least six weeks' notice if possible.)

## Sources

We owe a great debt to Wikipedia, which is our first stop for research. We attempt to make independent confirmation of all important dates and facts through a variety of other sources. Other sources we frequently use include the Library of Congress; "on this day" listings from *Encyclopedia Britannica*, the *New York Times*, and the BBC; Omniglot for the names of months in other languages; *Chase's Calendar of Events;* and, of course, the always essential Google.

All art and photographs are either in the public domain, used under a Creative Commons license, or with a "fair use" justification, and most frequently come from Wikimedia Commons and the Library of Congress Prints and Photographs Division.

Attribution is provided where possible, or as requested by the copyright owner, or when there is particular historical significance, listed below. For information about any particular illustration or photograph, please contact us.

# Credits

- The photograph of a Halloween pumpkin lamp on the cover is by Bojan Cvetanović, and is used here under CC BY-SA 40.

- The painting of *October* on the back cover and in the "October in Other Languages" section is from the 15th century illuminated manuscript *Très Riches Heures du Duc de Berry* by the Limbourg brothers and Barthélemy d'Eyck. It is in the public domain because any copyright has expired.

- The 1912 Halloween card is by John Winsch, and is in the public domain because it was published before 1923.

- The "Halloween Precautions" postcard is from the collection of the New York Public Library. No known copyright restrictions exist.

- The photograph of a piece of art at the Musical Instrument Museum, Phoenix, Arizona, was taken by Frank Kovalchek and is used here under CC BY-SA 2.0.

- The portrait of Martin Luther by Lucas Cranach the Elder was painted in 1528, and can by found in the Veste Coberg castle in Germany. It is in the public domain because its copyright has expired.

- The illustration of a woman being levitated is from *Magic*, by Ellis Stanyon, published in 1910. It is in the public domain because its copyright has expired.

- The photograph of Benito Mussolini is in the public domain in Italy because it was an image of a person taken more than 20 years ago, under the Law for the Protection of Copyright and Neighbouring Rights (n.633, 22 April 1941).

- The illustration of the "Dowding System" for defensive air control in the Battle of Britain is from a 1941 Air Ministry pamphlet. It is in the public domain as a work created by the UK government.

- The 2006 photograph of maintenance workers on Mount Rushmore was taken by Jeff Waddell, who released it into the public domain. It has been cropped.

- The 1917 photograph of Turkish lancers west of Beersheba in Ottoman Palestine is from the Matson Photograph Collection at the Library of Congress. It has been cropped. There are no known copyright restrictions on this work.

- The manuscript of "On Looking Into Chapman's Homer" by John Keats was hand-written by the author in 1816. It is in the public domain because its copyright has expired.

- The portrait of John Keats by William Hilton the Younger was painted circa 1822 and is in the public domain because its copyright has expired. The original can be found in the collection of the National Portrait Gallery.

- The 1966 publicity photograph of Brian Piccolo of the Chicago Bears. is in the public domain because it was published in the United States between 1923 and 1977 without a copyright notice. Traditionally, publicity photos are not copyrighted because of the way they are intended to be used.

- The 1960s publicity photograph of Michael Landon. is in the public domain because it was published in the United States between 1923 and 1977 without a copyright notice. Traditionally, publicity photos are not copyrighted because of the way they are intended to be used.

- The 1969 photograph of astronaut Michael Collins suiting up for the Apollo 11 mission is in the public domain as a work created by NASA.

- The 1970s photograph of Roy Rogers and Dale Evans at Knott's Berry Farm is from the Orange County Archives. No known copyright restrictions exist for this image.

- The photograph of Juliette Gordon Low at the 1923 Girl Scout Convention is from Underwood and Underwood, New York. Although it was copyrighted, the copyright was not renewed and the image is now in the public domain.

- The photograph of Ethel Waters is by William P. Gottlieb. It is from the William P. Gottlieb Collection at the Library of Congress. In accordance with the wishes of William Gottlieb, the photographs in this collection entered into the public domain on February 16, 2010.

- The letter challenging Houdini was created by John Heywood Ltd., Printers, Manchester, UK, circa 1904. It is in the public domain because its copyright has expired. It is part of the McManus-Young Collection at the Library of Congress.

- The 1919 photograph of Harry Houdini in chains is in the public domain because its copyright has expired. It is part of the McManus-Young Collection at the Library of Congress.

- The 1996 photograph of Indira Gandhi at the National Press Club in Washington, DC, is by Warren K. Leffler, *U. S. News and World Report*. It is part of the *U. S. News and World Report* Collection at the Library of Congress. Per the deed of gift, *U.S. News & World Report* dedicated to the public all rights it held for the photographs in this collection upon its donation to the Library.

- The 1898 photograph of Harry Houdini in chains from Lasky Corporation's "Famous Players" is in the public domain because its copyright has expired. It is part of the McManus-Young Collection at the Library of Congress.

- The 1921 advertisement for *Seven Years Bad Luck* appeared in the Jan-Jun 1921 run of *The Film Daily*. It is in the public domain because it was first published prior to 1923.

- The illustration "October" by Hans Thoma is from his book *Festkalender*. As the artist died in 1924, the work is in the public domain because its copyright has expired.

- The 1896 postcard of October is by Eugène Grasset. It is in the public domain because its copyright has expired.

- The painting *October* by Joachim von Sandrart was created prior to 1688, and is in the public domain because its copyright has expired. The original can be found at Schlossanlage Schleißheim, near München, Germany.

- The graphic of "Why" in several languages was created in 2011 by "Maierstrahl," and is used here under CC BY-SA 3.0.
- The advertisement for lucky jewelry appeared in a 1926 issue of *Art and Beauty* magazine. It is in the public domain because was published in the US more than 70 years ago with no statement of copyright.
- The painting *Marigolds* by Dante Gabriel Rossetti was created in 1873 and is in the public domain because its copyright has expired. The original can be found in the Castle Museum and Art Gallery, Nottingham, UK.
- The graphic "October" is credited to Morburre, who made it available under CC BY-SA 3.0.
- The celestial sphere is from *Scenography of the Ptolemaic Cosmography*, by Johannes van Loon, based on Andreas Cellarius's *Harmonia Macrocosmica*, 1660. It is in the public domain because its copyright has expired.
- The 1906 automobile calendar is by Edward Penfield, and is in the collection of the Library of Congress Prints and Photographs Division. It is in the public domain because its copyright has expired.
- The 50-year perpetual calendar photograph is in the public domain.
- The cartoon by John T. McCutcheon is from his 1905 collection *The Mysterious Stranger and Other Cartoons by John T. McCutcheon*. It is in the public domain because its copyright has expired.

# License Description and Terms

Aside from material purely in the public domain, photographs and other material in this book are used under specific licenses permitting free use, usually with an attribution requirement. For full text and terms of these licenses, click or enter the appropriate links below. If you believe there is an error in the copyright status or attribution of any of these images, please email us.

Michael Dobson

Timespinner
Press

# Other Books from Timespinner Press

### *The Story of a Special Day*
*Michael Dobson*

A series of (eventually) 366 volumes covering everything that happened on your special day! Events, births, deaths, quotes, holidays, and much more. It's like a birthday card they'll never throw away! Don't see your date available yet? Just write us!

US$7.95 print/US$2.99 ebook.

### *From Plassey to Pakistan*
*Humayun Mirza*

The history of British Colonial India and the formation of Pakistan from the unique perspective of the son of Pakistan's first president and last of the royal line of Bengal, Bihar, and Orissa! This unique historical document tells the inside story of this distinguished family, including the detailed story of the coup that toppled his father from power!

US$27.95 print

### *A Whole New Navy: America's War in the Pacific*

*Miles Durr*

The most comprehensive and detailed description of America's naval war in the Pacific ever—every battle, every ship, every task force and every task group from Pearl Harbor through the Japanese surrender! A must-have for the collection of every World War II buff!

US$29.95 print

### *Improbable History: The Weird, the Obscure, and the Strangely Important*

*edited by Michael Dobson*

From the birth of Western civilization to the rescue of Apollo 13, from the Leaning Tower of Pisa to Florence's Duomo, history has often turned on small, improbable details. Whatever happened to the ancient Samaritan people? Why did a fortuitous rainstorm allow the British to conquer India? How did an air raid in Italy lead to the development of chemotherapy? What happened when Albert Einstein met Adolf Hitler on the streets of Berlin? How did the Japanese manage to attack the US mainland using balloons? A cast of award-winning writers tackle some of the strangest tales in history!

US$19.95 print